SCIENCE 809
Balance In Nature

W9-AVA-622

LIFEPAC Test is located in the center of the booklet. Please remove before starting the unit.

Author:
Darnelle Dunn, M.S.Ed.

Editor-In-Chief:
Richard W. Wheeler, M.A.Ed.

Editor:
Lee H. Dunning, M.S.T., M.S.Ed.

Consulting Editor:
Harold Wengert, Ed.D.

Revision Editor:
Alan Christopherson, M.S.

Westover Studios Design Team:
Phillip Pettet, Creative Lead
Teresa Davis, DTP Lead
Nick Castro
Andi Graham
Jerry Wingo
Don Lechner

Alpha Omega
PUBLICATIONS

804 N. 2nd Ave. E.
Rock Rapids, IA 51246-1759

Balance In Nature

Introduction

If you could step away from earth for a moment, as the astronauts have done, you could easily see that the earth is an isolated planet. This planet can function only if all its systems are kept in balance. The sun is the only source of energy entering the system. Plants capture solar energy and convert carbon dioxide and water into food. This food supplies animals who digest it and give off carbon dioxide. Great advances have been made in agriculture that would startle the food gatherers of the past.

The elements of the earth are constantly recycled. Each element is part of a system and is used over and over again. Nitrogen, water, carbon, and oxygen are elements in the main endless cycles that insure a constant supply for plant growth and animal nutrition. The decay cycle involves the breakdown of organic matter and prevents dead organic matter from stockpiling in the earth.

Natural controls keep animal and plant populations in balance. Humans have brought pressure on both the environment and the natural resources. They are the only species able to control the environment and to make decisions that will affect the future. Scientists and concerned citizens are searching for answers, and the Bible declares (Proverbs 29:18), "Where there is no vision the people perish...."

Objectives

Read these objectives. The objectives tell you what you will be able to do when you have successfully completed this LIFEPAC. When you have finished this LIFEPAC, you should be able to:

1. Explain the leaf structures involved in photosynthesis.

2. List the nine requirements for plant growth.

3. Write a balanced equation for photosynthesis.

4. List the three major advances of modern agriculture.

5. Describe the hybrid plants and tell why they are so important.

6. Tell why some people are hungry and what can be done to help solve the problems of hunger.

7. Describe the relationship between Rhizobium bacteria, legume plants, and soil fertility.

8. Name the two important groups of decomposers and tell two values of decay.

9. Describe how water is recycled through precipitation, ground water, and transpiration.

10. Describe how the carbon dioxide of animal respiration and the oxygen of photosynthesis are involved in a cycle.

11. Define ten ecological terms.

12. Cite four human pressures on the environment and give an example of each.

13. List eight natural resources and give one way of conserving each resource.

Survey the LIFEPAC. Ask yourself some questions about this study and write your questions here.

1. PHOTOSYNTHESIS AND FOOD

The earth is an isolated planet. Energy comes from the sun, but nothing else enters or leaves planet *Earth*. Plants are basic to the existence of animals. Plants can use the energy from the sun and can produce complex molecules that serve as food for all animals. Plants also provide a constant source of oxygen for animal respiration.

Great advances in agriculture have been made since ancient people gathered berries and roots for survival. Today food production has increased with the use of machinery, farm chemicals, and **hybrid** plants. Scientists are constantly searching for improved techniques. Not all nations share equally in this new technology.

SECTION OBJECTIVES

Review these objectives. When you have completed this section, you should be able to:

1.   Explain the leaf structures involved in photosynthesis.

2.   List the nine requirements for plant growth.

3.   Write a balanced equation for photosynthesis.

4.   List the three major advances of modern agriculture.

5.   Describe hybrid plants and tell why they are so important.

6.   Tell why some people are hungry and what can be done to help solve the problems of hunger.

VOCABULARY

Study these words to enhance your learning success in this section.

catalyst (kat′ u list). A substance that brings about a change without being altered.

chlorophyll (klôr′ u fil). The green pigment found in most plants.

chloroplast (klôr′ u plast). A special cell body containing chlorophyll.

epidermis (ep′ u dėr′ mis). The outer layer of cells on the leaf.

glucose (glü′ kōs). The simple sugar formed during photosynthesis.

guard cell (gärd sel). A special cell that regulates the stomata.

hybrid (hī′ brid). The result of a cross between two unlike animals or plants.

photosynthesis (fō′ tu sin′ thu sis). The process of plants converting carbon dioxide and water into glucose and oxygen.

protein (prō′ tēn). An organic molecule containing nitrogen.

starch (stärch). A chain of simple sugar units.

stoma (plural stomata) (stō′ mu). Small pore in a leaf.

sugar (shug' ur). A simple organic compound of carbon, hydrogen, and oxygen such as the glucose molecule produced in photosynthesis.

trace elements (trās el' u munts). A group of elements that are needed in very small amounts for plant growth.

transpiration (tran' spu rā' shun). The loss of water through stomata.

Note: *All vocabulary words in this LIFEPAC appear in* **boldface** *print the first time they are used. If you are not sure of the meaning when you are reading, study the definitions given.*

Pronunciation Key: hat, āge, cãre, fär; let, ēqual, tėrm; it, īce; hot, ōpen, ôrder; oil; out; cup, put, rüle; child; long; thin; /ŦH/ for then; /zh/ for measure; /u/ represents /a/ in about, /e/ in taken, /i/ in pencil, /o/ in lemon, and /u/ in circus.

PHOTOSYNTHESIS

Photosynthesis is a complex chemical reaction that takes place mainly in the leaves of plants. Special bodies called **chloroplasts** contain the **chlorophyll** necessary for energy absorption.

The Structure. The leaf is the basic center for photosynthesis. Most leaves are flat with a large surface area. Leaves are also often oriented to the sun to capture available light. The surface, or **epidermal** layer, of leaf cells is covered with a waxy layer that reduces water loss. Photosynthesis occurs in the inner cells of the leaf where the chlorophyll is found.

Chlorophyll is the green pigment found in the interior cells of most leaves. It acts as a **catalyst** during photosynthesis. A catalyst is a substance that changes the rate of a reaction without being altered itself. Chlorophyll is responsible for absorbing energy from light and passing it through a cycle. This cycle converts the energy into a form the plant can use and store. Chlorophyll is located in small cell bodies called chloroplasts. Chloroplasts are found in the interior cells of leaves and in one type of surface cell.

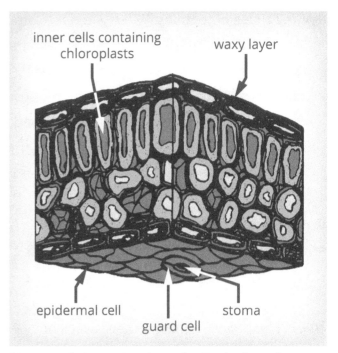

Figure 1 | Cross Section of a Typical Leaf

Plants can also have orange and yellow pigments. In the autumn chlorophyll is no longer produced by the leaf; therefore, the yellow and orange pigments show through. Some leaves also produce a red pigment under cool fall conditions. This pigment gives the typical red autumn color of maples and sumacs.

Try this investigation.

These supplies are needed:

- eye dropper
- microscope
- leaves from two unlike plants
- new single-edged razor blade
- cover slip
- glass slide
- water

Leaf 1

Follow these directions and complete the activities.
Put a check in the box when each step is completed.

☐ 1. Roll a leaf lengthwise into a tight roll.

☐ 2. Carefully cut thin slices of the leaf roll. Make some slices so thin that you almost end up with nothing.

☐ 3. Mount the thinnest pieces in water. Drop on the glass slide and cover with a cover slip. The leaf sections should look like tiny threads. If they are larger, keep slicing until you have thinner pieces.

Leaf 2

☐ 4. Search through the microscope until you find a section that looks like Figure 1.

1.1 In the space provided, Leaf 1, draw what you see.

☐ 5. Repeat Steps 1 through 4 using a leaf from another type of plant.

1.2 Draw the second leaf in the space, Leaf 2, provided.

TEACHER CHECK _____ _____
initials   date

Leaf Structure Experiment

Complete these sentences.

1.3 Leaves have a waxy coating to _____ .

1.4 Chlorophyll is found in small packets called _____ .

1.5 Plant pigments can be of four colors: a. _____ , b. _____ ,

c. _____ , and d. _____ .

Stomata (singular: stoma) are openings in the leaf surface, mainly on the underside. Carbon dioxide enters the leaf through the stomata, and water and oxygen escape through the stomata. A leaf may have 300,000 stomata. Two special cells called **guard cells** control the size of the opening. Unlike other leaf epidermal cells, guard cells do have chlorophyll. When light strikes the chloroplasts of the guard cells, the cells bow and an opening develops (Figure 2). Carbon dioxide can now enter the cell and photosynthesis occurs. When the light is gone, the guard cells shrink and come together. The stoma is now closed. The stomata also closes when conditions are dry.

Water vapor escapes from the leaf also through the stomata. This water loss is called **transpiration**. On a warm day a corn plant loses as much as two liters of water. Evaporation of the water provides a cooling system for the plant. The plant may die if high temperatures continue for long or if no soil moisture is available to replace lost water.

Desert plants have a variety of adaptations to combat the loss of water through transpiration. Desert shrubs have small leaves with few stomata. Other desert plants form leaves only when sufficient moisture is available for growth. They drop their leaves when the soil becomes dry. Cacti have only spiny leaves and carry on photosynthesis in their thickened stems.

Plants need light, water, carbon, hydrogen, oxygen, nitrogen, phosphorus, potassium, and about ten other chemical elements. The carbon comes from the carbon dioxide of the air.

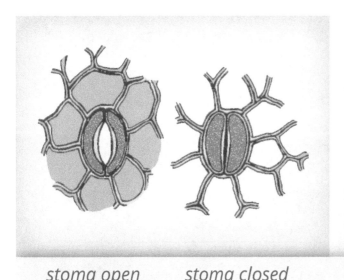

stoma open   *stoma closed*

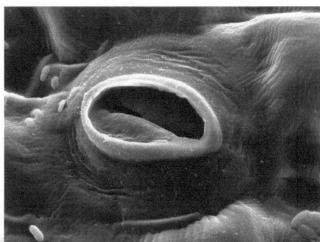

tomato leaf stoma

Figure 2 | Guard Cells

Oxygen comes both from the atmosphere and from the water molecule. Hydrogen is obtained from water; and nitrogen, from compounds produced by soil bacteria. Phosphorus and potassium are found in the soil along with the ten other elements. The ten additional elements are only needed in trace amounts and are called **trace elements**. Most soils are not lacking in trace elements.

The three elements commonly lacking in cultivated soil are nitrogen, phosphorus, and potassium. These three elements are added to the soil by using artificial fertilizer. Nitrogen, phosphorus, and potassium are always listed in the same order on any fertilizer package. A label that lists 30-19-11 means that the product contains 30 percent nitrogen, 19 percent phosphorus, and 11 percent potassium. The consumer is expected to know the order of the elements and that the numbers indicate percent. Nitrogen is necessary for green foliage and rapid plant growth. Phosphorus encourages strong roots and stems. Potassium aids the plant in disease resistance.

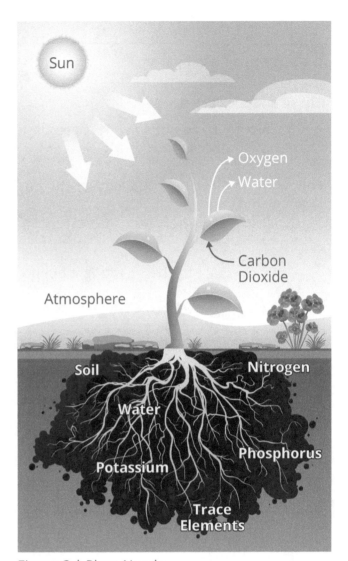

Figure 3 | Plant Needs

Try this investigation.

These supplies are needed:

- 250-milliliter beaker of freshly picked leaves
- clear plastic bag to hold the leaves
- fastener

Follow these directions and answer the questions. Put a check in the box when each step is completed.

☐ 1. Place the leaves in the plastic bag and close securely.

☐ 2. Place the bag in the light but not in the hot sun.

☐ 3. Observe at the end of twenty-four hours.

1.6   What happened inside the bag? _____

_____

1.7   What plant process does this change demonstrate? _____

1.8   How did the water escape from the leaves? _____

_____

1.9   What result would you have expected if you had put a cactus plant in the bag? _____

_____

1.10   Why are cacti adapted to low water loss? _____

_____

Transpiration Experiment

✎ Answer this question by matching the following items. Where do plants obtain these requirements?

1.11 _____ carbon   a. sun

1.12 _____ hydrogen   b. precipitation

1.13 _____ oxygen   c. carbon dioxide

1.14 _____ nitrogen   d. bacterial action in soil

1.15 _____ trace elements   e. carbon dioxide and atmosphere

1.16 _____ water   f. water molecule

1.17 _____ light   g. soil

                                   h. chlorophyll

Answer these questions.

1.18 Where are stomata found? _____

1.19 What cells regulate the opening and closing of the stomata? _____

1.20 What may happen if plants have no soil moisture? _____

_____

1.21 What is the purpose of stomata? _____

_____

1.22 How do cacti survive in the desert? _____

_____

1.23 Three elements are commonly found in bags of fertilizer. What are they and what does each do for the plant.

a. _____   _____

b. _____   _____

c. _____   _____

Complete these sentences.

1.24 Water escaping from a leaf through the stomata is called _____ .

1.25 Elements that are needed by a plant in very small amounts are called

_____ .

1.26 The common green pigment found in plants is called _____ .

1.27 Leaves are usually thin and flat to provide _____ .

1.28 Desert shrubs' leaves are adapted to the dry climate by having very few _____ .

The chemistry. For centuries no one understood photosynthesis. People assumed that plants grew by extracting material from the soil. The first scientific experiment to investigate plant growth was done by Van Helmont (1577-1644) in the early seventeenth century. He potted a young willow in a container of soil after carefully weighing the tree and the soil. For five years this Belgian scientist faithfully cared for the willow. He gave it only rain water. Five years later Van Helmont removed the willow from the soil and reweighed the tree and the soil. The willow had gained 72 kilograms but the soil had lost .057 kilograms. The loss by the soil was not enough to account for even a fraction of the increase in willow. Van Helmont incorrectly assumed that the increase in plant material came from the rain water. This experiment was a start in the search for an explanation of plant growth.

Scientist are still studying the chemistry of photosynthesis, but the general framework is understood. Plants convert carbon dioxide and water into a simple **sugar** using light as the energy source and chlorophyll as the catalyst.

Six molecules of carbon dioxide from the air are combined with twelve molecules of water. Light acts as the energy source, and chlorophyll is the energy absorber for the formation of one molecule of **glucose** (a simple sugar) and six molecules of oxygen. The oxygen is considered a waste product and leaves the plant through the stomata, see Equation 1.

Photosynthesis occurs in two steps. The first step requires light and is often called the *light phase*. When light strikes a molecule of chlorophyll, the molecule is changed slightly. This changed molecule is able to split water into hydrogen and oxygen. Ions are atoms or groups of atoms that have lost or gained electrons which gives the particles an electric charge. A new form of energy is produced that can be stored later in the reaction. When the water molecule is split, the oxygen is released from the plant; but the hydrogen remains. This oxygen is very important to the animal life of our planet. Plants are the only common source of atmospheric oxygen on our planet.

The second step of photosynthesis does not require light and is called the *dark phase* even though it can and does also occur in the light. The energy has already been absorbed by the chlorophyll. The reaction can continue whether or not light is currently available. The stored energy from the first step now allows the carbon dioxide to react with the hydrogen ions to form glucose and water. Water is the waste product of the second step and escapes from the plant through the stomata. The carbon dioxide in the atmosphere is a product of animal respiration. Plants could not live without animals to produce the carbon dioxide.

Equation 1: Total Photosynthesis

$$6\ CO_2 + 12\ H_2O \xrightarrow[Chlorophyll]{Light} C_6H_{12}O_6 + 6\ O_2 + 6\ H_2O$$

Equation 2: The Light Phase

$$2\ H_2O \xrightarrow[Chlorophyll]{Light\ activated} 4\ H^+ + O_2$$

Equation 3: The Dark Phase

$$6\ CO_2 + 24\ H^+ \rightarrow C_6H_{12}O_6 + 6\ H_2O$$

Photosynthesis

Glucose is a simple sugar that is easily converted to **starch**. Starch is a long chain of these simple sugar units. Starch is stored in the leaf temporarily. In the dark phase starch is converted back into glucose and is transported to the storage areas of the plant.

A variety of plant parts serve as storage areas. Roots, leaves, stems, fruits, tubers, flowers, and seeds can all be used by the plant as reservoirs of food. Glucose can be converted to other compounds in the final storage area.

Starch is a common storage chemical of vegetables such as potatoes and corn. A complex sugar called *sucrose* is abundant in sugar cane, where it is concentrated in the stem. In sugar beets sucrose is formed and stored in the root. These two plants are used as commercial sources of common table sugar. Many ripe fruits contain sucrose and other sugars, which give them their sweet taste.

Seeds and nuts were highly prized by ancient people as well as by modern man. Seeds and nuts are high in **protein**, fats, and oils. Proteins are organic molecules containing nitrogen. Animals need protein to build their own cells and must obtain their protein requirements from plants or other animals. Fats and oils are high in energy. They yield about twice as much energy by weight as sugars or starches yield.

 Complete the chart. Use a dictionary or ask your parent. Each of the following plants stores food that is used as food by humans. Put a check in the column that indicates what part of the plant is served as food. (The chart is continued on the next page.)

1.29	leaf	fruit	seed	stem	flower	root	tuber
a. carrot							
b. cabbage							
c. cauliflower							
d. coconut							
e. rhubarb							
f. beet							
g. artichoke							
h. wheat							
i. cherry							
j. corn							
k. sugar cane							
l. spinach							

	leaf	fruit	seed	stem	flower	root	tuber
m. yam							
n. radish							
o. asparagus							
p. broccoli							
q. pea							
r. potato							

Complete these activities.

1.30 Pretend that you are the engineer appointed to design a spaceship that will be gone from the earth for twenty years. Food will have to be grown on the ship. No supplies can be brought to the ship once it leaves the earth. The spaceship will be completely sealed so that you will have to provide carbon dioxide, oxygen, and water. In your best English write a 500-word theme about your design.

TEACHER CHECK _____ _____
                                    initials   date

Match these items.

1.31 _____ fruit

1.32 _____ nuts and seeds

1.33 _____ vegetables

1.34 _____ fats and oils

1.35 _____ dark phase

1.36 _____ light phase

1.37 _____ starch

1.38 _____ glucose

1.39 _____ sun

1.40 _____ oxygen

1.41 _____ carbon dioxide

a. oxygen released

b. source of all energy

c. simple sugar

d. complex sugar

e. high energy

f. epidermal waxy coat

g. source of starch

h. oils, fats, and proteins

i. source of carbon in photosynthesis

j. a chain of simple sugar units

k. necessary for animal respiration

l. water released

Complete this activity.

1.42 Complete this equation and balance it.

$$\underline{\hspace{4cm}} + \underline{\hspace{4cm}} \quad \longrightarrow \quad C_6H_{12}O_6 + \underline{\hspace{3cm}} + \underline{\hspace{3cm}}$$

Answer these questions.

1.43 What is the source of the carbon in glucose? _____

1.44 What is the energy source for photosynthesis? _____

1.45 Why are animals so important to plants? _____

1.46 Where does the carbon dioxide in the air come from? _____

_____

1.47 What would happen to plants if all of the animals in the world should die?

_____

1.48 What two things would happen to animals if all the plants in the world should disappear?

a. _____

b. _____

FOOD

In the past, food was often scarce and of poor quality. Ancient people had to spend much time and energy avoiding starvation. Modern agriculture has solved the food problems in advanced countries. Inventors and scientists have developed machines, chemicals, and hybrid plants that make food production more efficient. Unfortunately, these advances have not spread to all nations.

Food production in the past. At the Creation, God provided food for mankind and animals. He gave the green plants for their food (Genesis 1:29, 30). In the Garden of Eden, food was plentiful and easily obtained. After sin entered the world, the ground was cursed, thorns and thistles grew, and people would have to work hard to get their food (Genesis 3:17-19). Cain was a tiller of the ground, and Abel kept a flock of sheep, possibly for sacrifices.

After the Flood, in addition to plants for food, God also gave the people meat (Genesis 9:2-4). Animals, birds, and fish became fearful of people. Human beings could grow fruit and vegetables in their own fields and hunt animals for food. Animals were domesticated and raised for food.

In some areas people had to move often in search for food. Some people settled near rivers and lakes because fish were easier to catch and were a more reliable food source than animals.

Although most plants store food somewhere in their tissues, the food is not always in a form usable by humans. The cell walls of plants cannot be digested in the human stomach. Grass is often abundant, but it is not a human food for this reason.

Food gathering and ancient farming could not support many people. The basic principles of plant and animal breeding and agricultural practices were not known until the late nineteenth and twentieth centuries. Farmers could only use trial and error in choosing which animals to pick for reproduction.

Complete this chart. Compare your life with the life of someone of your own age who lived in ancient times.

		You	Ancient Friend
1.49	dinner	a.	b.
1.50	clothing	a.	b.
1.51	education	a.	b.
1.52	recreation	a.	b.
1.53	possessions	a.	b.
1.54	transportation	a.	b.
1.55	health	a.	b.

Food production today. The Industrial Revolution of the nineteenth century brought about a major change in agriculture. Crop production was slow and depended upon heavy hand labor. Beginning in the 1860s, machines such as McCormick's reaper were invented. That machine did the work of eight people. Soon other machines were developed for almost every aspect of agriculture. Farmers could cultivate and harvest larger fields in a fraction of the time formerly required.

Trains could transport machines from factories to the farms. Crops could be quickly transported back to the cities. Now cattle and crops could be raised in suitable areas miles away and be brought into the populated areas to be sold. Farming changed from being a family growing food only for home use into a larger business operation. Then a family might sell the entire crop or herd each year and consume only a small portion of the harvest on the farm.

Today, the farmer has an array of chemicals that can kill insects (insecticides), kill weeds (herbicides), and supply nutrients to the crops (fertilizers). The wise use of chemicals can greatly increase crop yields.

Before modern agriculture the only way to grow more food was to put more land into cultivation. The development of machinery, chemicals, and hybrid plants meant that fewer people could grow more food in less time without needing any additional ground.

The role of the scientist in food production. Gregor Mendel, an Austrian monk, carried out extensive plant breeding experiments in the 1860s. He used garden peas to investigate the laws of inheritance. People had always thought that all plant characteristics always showed up in the plant. Mendel showed that this hypothesis was wrong by crossing two garden pea plants. He used one plant that produced green peas and another that yielded yellow peas. All the resulting plants had yellow pea seeds. Now he crossed two of these new plants and found that their offspring varied. Three-fourths of the

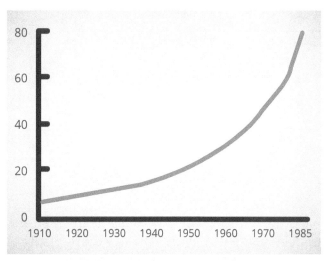

Figure 4 | The Number of People Fed by One United States Farmer

plants had yellow peas and one-fourth of the plants had green peas. Somehow the factor for green peas had been hidden in the yellow peas for generations. This experiment showed that plants could carry characteristics that were not apparent in the plants. Unfortunately, Mendel's work remained unknown and undiscovered until about 1900.

Luther Burbank (1849-1926) was a devoted plant breeder whose efforts gave the world over eight hundred new varieties of plants. He was not a trained scientist, but he did use basic scientific principles. The findings of Mendel were not available to him when he started his work. Burbank was born in Massachusetts, and his first plant success was a new potato. He sold the seeds of this potato to finance his move to California. There he operated a research farm at Santa Rosa. He hybridized thousands of plants. Burbank once selected 30,000 plum trees from which 113 were worthy of further investigation. One of his unusual accomplishments was a plum without a pit.

Complete this activity.

1.56 Look up Luther Burbank in the encyclopedia or online and make a list of five plants that he developed. Write them in the space provided.

a. _____   b. _____

c. _____   d. _____

e. _____

A plant geneticist works with plants in an effort to develop new varieties. Usually these plants are hybrids, which are the result of crossing two different strains. Such plants often are stronger and more vigorous than the scientist expected them to be. This extra quality is called *hybrid vigor*. This phenomenon cannot be explained but does result in plants that are stronger, give better yields, and are more disease resistant. New seeds must be purchased each year. A hybrid is a cross between two known, but unlike, strains; therefore, the seeds produced by the hybrid plant would be either self-pollinated or of unknown pollination. The added cost of new seed each year is worth the expense because the hybrid plant produces a larger crop per acre.

Geneticists breed animals as well as plants. In both cases geneticists are looking for one or more of three objectives. *First,* in almost every case the scientists are striving for a greater yield of edible food. In plants a greater yield could mean larger fruit or more seeds. In animals more meat or eggs are sought. *Second,* improvement in quality is a goal. Farmers and consumers hope for more tender beef or sweeter fruit. *Third,* each plant has some special characteristic that the geneticist hopes to incorporate. Perhaps the crop grows well in a certain area, but frost in that area kills the plant before the crop can be harvested. The search is then begun for a variety that will mature faster. Sometimes an area is infested with a plant disease, and a variety must be found that is resistant. At times researchers develop some unusual plants or animals. Argentine plant breeders claim to have developed a strain of corn that has such bitter-tasting leaves that grasshoppers refuse to eat the plant.

The development of hybrid corn is a plant success story. Corn is native to the New World. Ancient corn was a tiny cob of just over two centimeters with about forty or fifty tiny kernels. Native American farmers selected the best ears for use as seed and, by the time Columbus arrived, corn was ten centimeters long. Columbus took samples back to his queen, but she was not interested.

Farmers did try raising the new crop, and eventually it spread around the world. By the early 1920s farmers in the United States were harvesting 25 bushels per acre. After hybrids were developed, the yield jumped to 50 bushels and then to 70 bushels. Corn yields have increased more than 300 percent per acre since the 1930s.

The original wheat of the Tigris River area was nothing more than a wild grass. Kernel production was low and the wheat easily fell off the plant. Farmers selected plants at random to use as seed for the next crop. Production did increase, but still the seeds fell off shortly after the grain ripened. Farmers planted no more wheat than the family and hired workers could harvest in the few short days. McCormick's reaper increased the amount of wheat that could be harvested in a short time. Today new hybrids of wheat are available that hold the grain more firmly to the stalk until harvesting.

The International Rice Research Institute in the Philippines has led the way in the search for hybrid rice. Rice is the basic food of Asia and is commonly eaten in Africa and South America. Besides searching for hybrids that will give greater yields, researchers are looking for a plant that is shorter and stiffer. Current crops are often lost when winds blow the plants over to the ground. Some experimental plots using hybrid rice plants, fertilizer, and insecticides have given yields four times greater than was possible with old strains and methods.

 Complete these activities.

1.57 Many religious and governmental groups are involved in providing food for the hungry. Some groups deal with local hunger; others, with problems abroad. Find out about one group that helps the hungry. Share your findings with five classmates. Lead a short discussion about hunger and what Christians can do to help.

TEACHER CHECK _____ _____
                                                  initials   date

1.58 List the three common goals of plant- and animal-breeding experiments.

a. _____

b. _____

c. _____

1.59 List two special characteristics that scientists could look for in breeding plants.

a. _____

b. _____

The problems of world food production. The amount of food produced on our planet has remained rather stable in recent years, but our world population has soared. Two babies are born every second. Most of these babies are from underdeveloped lands where food production is low. Africa, Asia, Central and South America are not self-sufficient. They must rely on imports to fill their food needs. Food is being constantly shipped in from stockpiles in developed nations. A drought, flood, or other disaster in the food-producing nations could cause a major problem in food distribution. Each country must work to become self-sufficient. Our responsibility is to share the Gospel with the world (Matthew 28:19, 20). Our earthly goods are to be shared with fellow Christians. "But whoso hath this world's goods, and seeth his brother have need, and shutteth up his bowels of compassion from him, how dwelleth the love of God in him" (1 John 3:17).

In many underdeveloped countries, agricultural practices have been the same for hundreds of years. Education is necessary to show people how to use the appropriate fertilizers, pesticides, and hybrids suitable for their crops, climate, and soil. In desert regions, wells and irrigation are needed to supply water before crops can be grown at all. Insects, plant disease, and rats are estimated to ruin one-third of the harvest in some areas. Other lands have been farmed for centuries and the soil nutrients are gone. Proper fertilization and hybrid plants could easily multiply crop yields.

Most world crops are composed mainly of starch and sugars. These foods provide calories, vitamins, and minerals; but humans also require protein. Beans, nuts, and seeds provide protein; but animal foods are the most complete source. When grain is scarce, there is wisdom in feeding it to people and not to animals. Fifteen pounds of plant material is required to produce one pound of beef. A ten-acre plot could support eight people if the land were used to raise beef; twenty people could be fed if corn were planted; and thirty-five, if rice were grown. Many more people can be fed if land is planted in grains that are eaten directly by people even though protein from animals is important for good health. You have probably

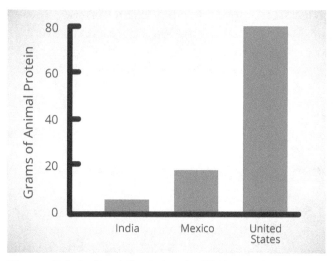

Figure 5 | Animal Proteins in Diet

seen pictures of children with swollen stomachs, thin arms, and discolored hair. They are suffering from a lack of protein. This condition often results in a mental disability. The children are so weakened that any illness or infection can be fatal.

Answer these questions.

1.60   Where was Gregor Mendel born? _____

1.61   When did Mendel make his study? _____

1.62   What natural laws did Mendel investigate? _____

1.63   Why was one of Burbank's plums unusual? _____

1.64   What is a hybrid? _____

_____

1.65   Why must new seeds be purchased each year if a farmer wishes to grow hybrid grain crops?

_____

_____

1.66   Why was wheat grown only in small amounts before machinery and hybrid seed?

_____

1.67   How did machinery and hybrid seeds help increase wheat production?

_____

_____

1.68   What is happening to the world population?   _____

1.69   What has been happening to world production?

_____

1.70   How many babies are born each second?   _____

1.71   What must be done to soil that is not fertile? _____

1.72   What items are often needed before crops can be grown in the desert lands?

a. _____

b. _____

1.73   Why is meat an important part of the diet of a human?   _____

_____

1.74   What are the symptoms that develop when a person has not been eating sufficient protein?
List four.

a. _____

b. _____

c. _____

d. _____

1.75   What amount of the crop is destroyed in some countries before it can be consumed by the

people? _____

Complete these activities.

1.76 Discuss the problems that your answers to Questions 1.68 to 1.75 are causing in the world.

_____

_____

_____

_____

_____

_____

1.77 On a separate sheet of paper draw both ancient and modern corn, life size. Use these sizes:

Ancient corn, 2 centimeters;
Corn that Columbus saw, 10 centimeters; and
Modern corn, 20 centimeters.

TEACHER CHECK _____ _____
                                         initials   date

1.78 Complete this chart.

Acres Farmed	Number of people that could be fed
10 acres used for beef raising	a.
10 acres planted in corn	b.
10 acres planted in rice	c.

Answer these questions.

1.79 Most world crops are of what two types of food? a. _____ and

b. _____ .

1.80 What do they (1.79) provide? a. _____ b. _____ c. _____

1.81 What basic human requirement do starches and sugars not provide in a complete form?

_____

Review the material in this section in preparation for the Self Test. The Self Test will check your mastery of this particular section. The items missed on this Self Test will indicate specific areas where restudy is needed for mastery.

SELF TEST 1

Write true or false (each answer, 1 point).

1.01 _____ Stems are the basic center for photosynthesis.

1.02 _____ Photosynthesis occurs in two steps.

1.03 _____ Transpiration is water loss through the root.

1.04 _____ The formula for glucose is $C_6H_{12}O_6$.

1.05 _____ When food is scarce, grain should be fed to animals and then the meat can be eaten.

1.06 _____ Carbon dioxide is the waste product of photosynthesis.

1.07 _____ Animals are the only common source of oxygen for plants.

1.08 _____ Mendel studied the law of inheritance.

1.09 _____ Protein is commonly lacking in the diet of underdeveloped nations.

1.010 _____ Chlorophyll is located in chloroplasts.

Match these items (each answer, 2 points).

1.011 _____ chlorophyll

1.012 _____ stomata

1.013 _____ starch

1.014 _____ cacti

1.015 _____ carbon dioxide

1.016 _____ fertilizer

1.017 _____ Mendel

1.018 _____ dark phase

1.019 _____ guard cell

1.020 _____ hybrid

a. regulates opening

b. cross between two unlike varieties

c. no leaves

d. source of carbon for plant

e. McCormick reaper

f. water released

g. green pigment

h. pea plants

i. pores in leaf

j. nutrients added to soil

k. chain of glucose units

Write the letter of the correct choice (each answer, 2 points).

1.021 The two waste products of photosynthesis are _____ .
a. water and oxygen
b. oxygen and hydrogen
c. carbon dioxide and water
d. glucose and oxygen

1.022 A typical leaf does *not* contain _____ .
a. chloroplasts
b. epidermal cells
c. guard cells
d. hybrids

1.023 Stomata are *not* used for _____ .
a. escape of water
b. escape of glucose
c. escape of oxygen
d. carbon dioxide collection

1.024 Plants need to be provided with all of the following items *except* _____ .
a. starch   b. trace minerals   c. light   d. water

1.025 The major elements found in commercial fertilizer are _____ .
a. oxygen, nitrogen, and carbon
b. phosphorus, hydrogen, and oxygen
c. nitrogen, potassium, and oxygen
d. nitrogen, phosphorus, and potassium

1.026 Stomata are found mainly on the _____ .
a. top of leaves
b. bottom of leaves
c. surface of all plant parts
d. bottom of all stems and roots

1.027 Plants are *not* good sources of _____ .
a. complete protein
b. complex sugars
c. starch
d. fats and oils

1.028 Hybrid plants are bred for _____ .
a. greater yields, taller stems, disease resistance
b. early maturity, better leaves, larger fruit
c. greater yield, increased quality, special characteristics
d. more seeds, increased quality, more tender beef

1.029 Most underdeveloped nations do *not* need _____ .
a. increased food production
b. hybrid plants
c. agricultural education
d. drought or flood

1.030 You could feed the most people if you used your land for _____ .
a. beef cattle   b. corn   c. rice   d. chickens

Complete these activities (each answer, 3 points).

1.031 Write the complete balanced equation for photosynthesis.

a. _____ + b. _____ c. $\longrightarrow$ d. _____ + e. _____

+ f. _____

1.032 List the three major contributions to modern agriculture.

a. _____ b. _____

c. _____

1.033 List the nine major requirements for plant growth.

a. _____ b. _____

c. _____ d. _____

e. _____ f. _____

g. _____ h. _____

i. _____

1.034 Name five plant storage organs and give an example of each.

a. _____ _____

b. _____ _____

c. _____ _____

d. _____ _____

e. _____ _____

2. NATURAL CYCLES

The existence of life on this planet depends on the constant recycling of many important elements. Nitrogen, carbon, oxygen, and water all have their own intricately balanced cycles. The process of decay contributes to each of these cycles and rids the earth of excessive organic matter.

SECTION OBJECTIVES

Review these objectives. When you have completed this section, you should be able to:

7. Describe the relationship between *Rhizobium* bacteria, legume plants, and soil fertility.

8. Name the two important groups of decomposers and tell two values of decay.

9. Describe how water is recycled through precipitation, ground water, and transpiration.

10. Describe how the carbon dioxide of animal respiration and the oxygen of photosynthesis are involved in a cycle.

VOCABULARY

Study these words to enhance your learning success in this section.

bacteria (bak tir′ ē u). Tiny single-celled plants.

decomposition (dē kom pu zish′ un). To decay, or rot.

fungi (fun′ jī). Members of the plant kingdom without chlorophyll.

legume (leg′ yüm). A group of plants that form root nodules.

nodule (noj′ ül). The enlargement on the root of a legume.

Rhizobium (rī zō′ bē um). The group of bacteria found in legume nodules.

THE NITROGEN CYCLE

Nitrogen is one of the major elements needed for plant growth. The atmosphere is a vast storehouse of nitrogen, but in its free state nitrogen is not available for plant use. A special relationship between bacteria and legumes is responsible for converting nitrogen into a usable form. Fungi and several other bacterial groups recycle the nitrogen found in plants and animals when the organism dies.

Nitrogen from the atmosphere. Since the atmosphere is 78 percent nitrogen plants would seem to have an abundant supply.

Unfortunately the nitrogen in the air is not in a form that the plant can absorb and use. A small amount of usable compounds is formed during thunderstorms when heat produced by lightning combines nitrogen and oxygen. Rain then washes these compounds into the soil. Gardeners claim plants experience a burst of growth after a thunderstorm due to these nitrogen compounds.

Most available nitrogen in the soil comes from the action of nitrifying, or nitrogen-fixing, bacteria. The bacteria are named Rhizobium after the two Greek words *rhizo*, meaning *root*, and *bio*, meaning *life*. *Rhizobium* bacteria have a special relationship with legumes. Common legumes include clover, beans, peas, alfalfa, and peanuts. The bacteria are found in the soil and burrow into the root of a legume. The plant responds by forming a growth called a **nodule** in that area of the root. The bacteria live in the nodule and consume sugar and starches stored there. The bacteria are able to convert nitrogen found between particles of soil into nitrogen compounds the plant can use. Legume plants use all the nitrogen they need; the remainder is released from the nodule and enters the surrounding soil. An estimated 45 kilograms per acre of nitrogen can be produced in a growing season. About two-thirds of the world's required nitrogen fertilizer is a result of these bacteria.

Nitrogen from organic material. The cycle of nitrogen use continues when an animal consumes a plant. Protein of the plant is broken down during digestion, and new proteins are formed that are characteristic of that particular animal. Any protein surplus is excreted as *urea*. When the urea reaches the soil, several other bacterial groups decompose it back into usable molecules and the plants begin the cycle again. In some areas the waste products of birds (guano) have formed thick layers where the birds roost. Guano is rich in nitrates and is mined and used as fertilizer.

Until the animal or plant dies, some nitrogen is tied up in the form of protein. Upon death the nitrogen is again returned to the soil by the process of decay.

Thomas Jefferson suggested that farmers alternate their crops between different fields each year. Many crops are heavy users of nitrogen. If a legume is planted in the soil every few years the fertility of the soil is greatly increased by the action of the nitrogen-fixing bacteria. Crop rotation is now a common practice used to increase yields on farms. In an effort to get the most benefit possible from legume crops, many farmers till the legume into the soil. It decays and enriches the soil even more. Since this practice is a way of fertilizing the land using green plants, the practice came to be known as *green manure*.

When legumes are planted on poor soil, enough of the *Rhizobium* bacteria may not be available to form sufficient nodules. Powders

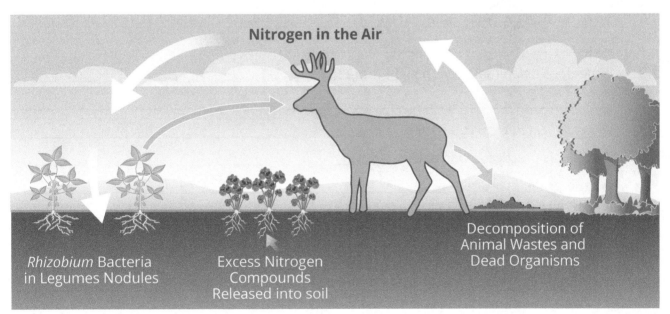

Nitrogen in the Air

Rhizobium Bacteria in Legumes Nodules

Excess Nitrogen Compounds Released into soil

Decomposition of Animal Wastes and Dead Organisms

Figure 6 | The Nitrogen Cycle

containing millions of these bacteria can be purchased and added during planting to insure a sufficient bacterial population. Some home gardeners regularly sprinkle this powder in the row when they plant pea and bean seeds. The bacterial action insures a better crop and enriches the garden soil for the next season.

Answer these questions.

2.1 Why are plants unable to use nitrogen from the air? _____

_____

2.2 What do *Rhizobium* bacteria do for legumes? _____

_____

2.3 What do legumes provide for *Rhizobium* bacteria? _____

_____

2.4 Where do nitrogen-fixing bacteria obtain nitrogen? _____

_____

2.5 What happens to the excess nitrogen compounds the legumes do not need?

_____

2.6 How much of the required world supply of nitrogen fertilizer is manufactured by legumes?

_____

2.7 What does an animal do with plant proteins? _____

_____

2.8 Who advocated crop rotation? a. _____ .

Why is this practice important? b. _____ .

2.9 What is green manure? _____

Complete this activity.

2.10 List the names of four legumes.

a. _____   b. _____

c. _____   d. _____

Complete this activity.

2.11 Find a farmer who can show you a legume root with nodules. Draw it and bring a sample to class. If this activity is not possible, consult an encyclopedia and write one paragraph about legume plants.

TEACHER CHECK _____ _____
initials   date

THE DECAY CYCLE

Decay is caused by a variety of organisms. At times decay is very damaging to food crops and wood but is necessary to keep the amount of organic matter on the earth at a manageable level.

The agents of decay. Eventually all plants and animals die and decay. A number of organisms are involved in the decay process, but most are either bacteria or fungi. Bacteria are single-celled organisms so small they can be seen only through a high-powered microscope. They cannot manufacture their own food and must obtain it from organic matter.

Fungi are simple members of the plant kingdom even though they do not have chlorophyll. They range from single cells up to large organisms measuring 50 centimeters or more. Since fungi have no chlorophyll they, too, need to obtain their food from other plant or animal material. Fungi can be of a wide variety of shapes and sizes.

Yeasts are one-celled fungi; certain strains are used in breadmaking and fermentation. The growths found on old bread and rotten fruit are common molds. Particular types give cheeses their distinctive flavors; one fungus is the source of penicillin. Mushrooms and puffballs are large fungi and usually obtain their nourishment from organic matter in the soil of moist areas. Bracket, or shelf, fungi are found on old stumps and logs.

Both bacteria and fungi are agents of decay and are found almost everywhere. When an animal or plant dies, **decomposition** begins. Decomposers use the nutrients in dead material as food for their own growth and reproduction. In the process they break down molecules into simpler units.

The value of decay. A vast amount of elements such as nitrogen, carbon, and trace minerals is tied up in living animals and plants. These elements are not released into the environment until after death and decomposition. Without this decay and release of valuable nutrients, life would eventually end. Plant growth would continue until the soil was depleted of its nutrients and then all growth would cease. Animals depend on plants for food and would continue eating until all the plants were gone. Soon the animals would starve. The cycle of life would end without the action of bacteria and fungi to release the critical elements back into the environment.

Besides recycling important nutrients, bacteria and fungi reduce the volume of organic matter produced each year. If leaves never decayed, the trees in a forest would soon be choked by their own leaves. If blades of grass did not decay, a lawn would smother itself. Many gardeners take organic material such as leaves, grass clippings, and vegetable peelings and put them in an area of their property to make a *compost* pile. If the pile is kept moist, the material decomposes. Compost makes a valuable addition to the garden soil. The nitrogen, carbon, and other elements contained in the compost are released and put back into the soil to start the cycle again.

The problem of decay. All decay is not economically valuable. Tons of fruits, vegetables, and grains decay each year before they can be sold or consumed. Wooden homes and fences in moist climates rot and must be replaced. Once animals are slaughtered the meat is good only for a short time.

Methods had to be found to preserve organic material from decomposition. Ancient people dried berries and meat. Even cooking is a form of preservation, although it extends the edible life only a few days. Salting was another easy

ancient method of preservation. Salt was so important in food preservation that people were paid wages in salt. This practice gave rise to the saying that a worker was "worth his salt."

Refrigeration and freezing slow down the growth of bacteria and fungi so that food can be stored for a longer period before spoiling. In canning, the food containers are heated to such high temperatures that the bacteria and fungi are killed. The food will stay free from decomposition as long as the seal is not broken. Nutritional values of canned foods decline with time, but the food remains edible. A meat roast canned in 1824 was opened 114 years later in 1938. The meat was fed to rats for ten days as an experiment. The rats remained alive and well.

Figure 7 | The Decay Cycle

SCIENCE 809

LIFEPAC TEST

NAME _____

DATE _____

SCORE _____

SCIENCE 809: LIFEPAC TEST

Match these items (each answer, 2 points).

1. _____ oxygen
2. _____ guard cells
3. _____ recycle
4. _____ carnivore
5. _____ glucose
6. _____ leaf
7. _____ root nodule
8. _____ decomposers
9. _____ greed
10. _____ habitat

a. simple sugar formed in photosynthesis
b. where an animal lives
c. to reuse old materials in making new
d. legume
e. eats only animals
f. waste product of photosynthesis
g. destroys rare animals and plants for profit
h. main center of photosynthesis
i. stomata
j. auto exhaust
k. fungi and bacteria

Write true or false (each answer, 1 point).

11. _____ Hybrid plants usually have increased vigor.
12. _____ Humans have destroyed natural controls out of ignorance.
13. _____ Trace elements always need to be added to the soil.
14. _____ Some carbon is tied up in fossil fuels.
15. _____ Modern agriculture is possible because of machines, farm chemicals, and hybrid plants.
16. _____ A scavenger eats only plant material.
17. _____ Greed, ignorance, technology, and population are all human disruptions of the environment.
18. _____ Most babies are born in lands of low-food production.
19. _____ Automobiles consume oxygen and give off 60 percent of the air pollution.
20. _____ In some areas of the world, one-third of the crop is destroyed before it can be eaten.

Write the letter of the correct answer on each line (each answer, 2 points).

21. Plants require light, carbon. hydrogen, oxygen, nitrogen, phosphorus, potassium, and
    _____ .
    a. water and trace elements
    b. nodules and sun
    c. water and *Rhizobium* bacteria
    d. trace elements and nodules

22. *Rhizobium* bacteria are important in soil fertility because plants _____ .
    a. cannot uses nitrogen from the air
    b. lack chloroplasts in the root
    c. cannot decompose nodules
    d. need the chlorophyll

23. Decomposition breaks down organic material into simpler units and _____ .
    a. rids the world of excess organic material
    b. rids the world of scavengers
    c. provides oxygen for photosynthesis
    d. provides proteins for plants

24. Plants and animals living together in an area make up a _____ .
    a. community   b. habitat   c. food chain   d. food

25. Carbon dioxide enters the leaf through _____ .
    a. epidermal cells   b. guard cells   c. stomata   d. root nodules

26. The capacity to alter the environment at will is a characteristic of _____ .
    a. decomposers   b. people   c. predators   d. scavengers

27. A cross between two unlike varieties gives a _____ .
    a. greater yield   b. natural control   c. waste product   d. hybrid

28. Soil, water, air, forests, minerals, fossil fuels, wildlife, and the wilderness are all examples
    of _____ .
    a. natural resources
    b. food pyramids
    c. agricultural advances
    d. technology

29. The diets of persons living in underdeveloped nations are usually lacking in _____ .
    a. grain   b. sugar   c. starch   d. protein

30. The only source of energy entering our earth is _____ .
    a. the sun   b. fossil fuels   c. water power   d. atomic energy

Match these items (each answer, 2 points).

31. _____ water table
32. _____ carbon dioxide
33. _____ ecology
34. _____ scavenger
35. _____ chloroplasts
36. _____ precipitation
37. _____ food preservation
38. _____ fossil fuel
39. _____ natural control
40. _____ producers

a. a body containing chlorophyll
b. all plants
c. eats dead material
d. plastics and energy
e. salt, dry, freeze
f. surface of ground water
g. condition that limits a population's growth
h. modern agriculture
i. relationship of organisms to environment
j. rain, snow, hail
k. produced during respiration

Answer these questions.

2.12 What are the two main groups of decomposers?

a. _____ b. _____

2.13 How do animals and plants contribute to the environment even after they die?

_____

_____

2.14 What would happen if no elements were ever recycled? _____

_____

2.15 Bacteria and fungi do not make their own food. Why? _____

_____

Complete these activities.

2.16 List five methods of food preservation. a. _____ b. _____

c. _____ d. _____ e. _____

2.17 List four commercial uses for fungi.

a. _____ b. _____

c. _____ d. _____

2.18 List two reasons that decomposition is so important.

a. _____

b. _____

2.19 Define *fungi.* _____

_____

2.20   Use the encyclopedia and write one paragraph about any one of these topics: penicillin, cheese manufacture, commercial mushroom growing. or Native American pemmican.

TEACHER CHECK _____ _____
                                                                            initials   date

2.21   OPTIONAL: Make up a story. Pretend no decay has taken place since time began. Every animal, plant, and person that has ever existed would still be here even though they are not alive. Be sure to stress the problems this situation would cause. Tell your tall tale to two friends. Have them initial this page.

HELPER CHECK _____ _____
                                                                  initials   date

HELPER CHECK _____ _____
                                                                  initials   date

THE WATER CYCLE

Water is the most common compound on earth. Moisture reaches earth in the form of precipitation, which eventually evaporates and recondenses in the upper atmosphere. The cycle is more complicated when the effects of ground water, transpiration, respiration, and polar ice are considered.

Precipitation cycle. A glance at a globe will show that water covers almost three-fourths of the surface of the earth. Water is our most abundant resource; however, without constant recycling land areas would be deserts. Water is constantly moving from the atmosphere to the earth and back to the atmosphere. This recycling is possible only because water is a unique substance that can easily change from gas to liquid to solid. Water reaches the earth as precipitation and flows into streams, rivers, and finally the oceans.

Solar radiation is the energy source for the evaporation and eventual return of water to the atmosphere. The rate of evaporation depends on the temperature of the air and water, the wind, and the amount of moisture already in the air. As the vapor rises, it reaches a point where the temperatures are cooler. There the vapor condenses on nuclei of dust. High-elevation wind currents may carry moisture thousands of kilometers before it is released as precipitation.

Total cycle. When precipitation reaches the earth, some of the water enters streams and rivers, but some sinks into the earth and becomes a part of the *ground water*. Ground water is stored in porous rocks and soil. The surface of this ground water is called the *water table*. In lakes and swamps the water table is above the surface of the ground. In other areas

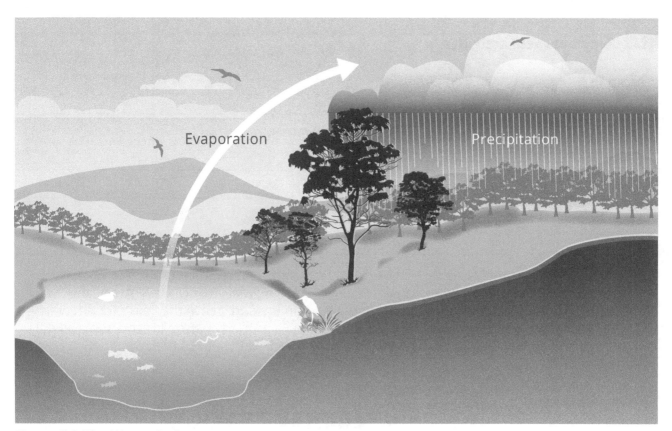

Figure 8 | The Water Cycle

the water table may be a few meters or even hundreds of meters beneath the surface.

If the water table is not too deep, some of the water moves up to the surface by capillary action. Capillary action is the upward movement of the water between the particles of soil. Water eventually reaches the root zone and is taken in by the plants. Water is then returned to the atmosphere by transpiration, which is a much faster process than evaporation. In the tropical rain forest, water is returned to the air so rapidly that the atmosphere above is constantly saturated. Rain showers occur almost daily.

Animals return water to the atmosphere through respiration, perspiration, and elimination. When you see your breath on a cold day, you are viewing the condensation of moisture as it escapes from your lungs. On a hot summer day you need to drink extra liquids to replace water lost by excessive perspiration. Survival books suggest that hikers carry at least one liter of water per person for each hour on the desert. Kidneys constantly filter blood and excrete waste and excess water in the urine. When animals (and plants) die, the cell moisture returns to the atmosphere during decomposition.

Varying amounts of water are trapped in polar ice. If the average temperature of the earth falls even slightly, the volume of polar ice increases and shorelines along the oceans drop. In warmer periods polar ice melts and coastal areas are flooded. These cycles are long and would not be noted in the lifetime of one person but do show that the amount of water on the planet is constant.

 Complete these activities.

2.22 List three forms of precipitation.

_____

2.23 List three factors on which the rate of evaporation depends.

_____

_____

2.24 List three ways animals return water to the atmosphere.

_____

2.25 Find a large, clear glass jar and construct a terrarium. Gather small plants from your yard or garden. Find a few crickets, snails, or other small animals to include. The soil should be barely moist. Place the jar in bright light but not in the sun. Leave the lid off for a few days if moisture starts to run down the sides of the jar. A properly balanced terrarium will only have a slight water vapor condensation during the coolest hour of the day.

TEACHER CHECK _____ _____
                                initials   date

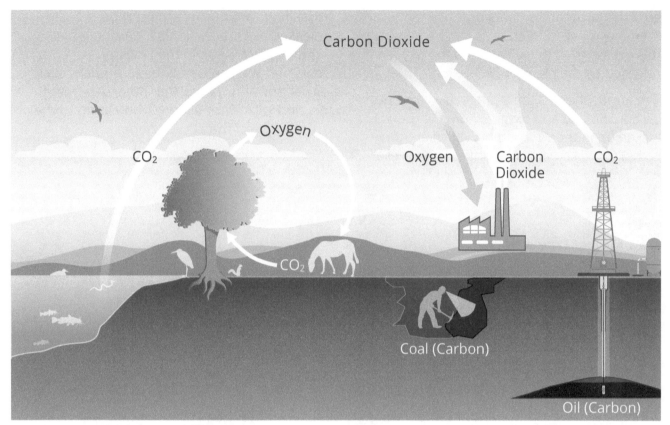

Figure 9 | The Carbon and Oxygen Cycle

THE CARBON AND OXYGEN CYCLE

Carbon and oxygen are often discussed together because they are so closely related. Carbon, in the form of carbon dioxide, is used in photosynthesis and is given off in respiration. Oxygen is used in respiration and is given off in photosynthesis.

The sun strikes the chlorophyll of plants and photosynthesis occurs. Carbon dioxide enters the stomata and oxygen is released. Animals and plants use the oxygen in respiration and excrete carbon dioxide. The same cycle occurs in a pond, lake, or balanced aquarium. Aquatic plants photosynthesize when light reaches them and give off oxygen, which is dissolved in the water. Fish, snails, and other aquatic animals and plants absorb the oxygen and release carbon dioxide. The plants absorb the carbon dioxide and the cycle continues.

In cold climates, ice covers the lakes and ponds in winter, but the process continues as long as sunlight penetrates the ice. If heavy snow covers the ice and prevents light from reaching the plants, the oxygen becomes depleted and the fish die. In spring when the ice melts, the shore is lined with dead fish from this winter kill. In some areas governmental or private groups interested in sport fishing will plow the snow off the ice. Sun can then reach the plants, and the carbon and oxygen cycles continue.

Oxygen is the waste product of photosynthesis; carbon dioxide is the waste product of respiration. Respiration is the process of utilizing the energy stored in food. Respiration occurs in both plants and animals. Plants manufacture food during photosynthesis but must utilize some of it to provide the energy for their growth. Fortunately plants produce more food than they need, and animals can benefit from this excess food as well as from the oxygen released by the plants.

The atmosphere is the storage area for both carbon dioxide and oxygen. Some carbon is locked up in the coal and oil, which are the compressed remains of plants. When these fossil fuels are burned, the carbon is again released as carbon dioxide. Carbon is also temporarily tied up in the limestone of coral reefs and the shells of aquatic animals, such as oysters and clams. With time, decay and erosion will return every carbon atom to the storehouse of the atmosphere.

Answer true or false.

2.26	_____	Transpiration is faster than evaporation.
2.27	_____	Carbon is sometimes locked up in nitrogen.
2.28	_____	Fish are healthier if snow covers the winter ice.
2.29	_____	Rate of evaporation depends on respiration.
2.30	_____	The water table is the surface of the lake.
2.31	_____	In warmer temperatures, shorelines of the ocean drop.
2.32	_____	Oxygen is a waste product of photosynthesis.
2.33	_____	The soil is the storage area for carbon dioxide and oxygen.
2.34	_____	Nitrogen is tied up in coral reefs.
2.35	_____	Plants provide food and oxygen for animal consumption.
2.36	_____	Life on earth would not be affected if decomposition should cease.

Complete this chart.

2.37

	Gas Required	Waste Product	Energy Source	Result
Photosynthesis	a.	b.	c.	d.
Respiration	a.	b.	c.	d.

Review the material in this section in preparation for the Self Test. This Self Test will check your mastery of this particular section as well as your knowledge of the previous section.

SELF TEST 2

Write true or false (each answer, 1 point).

2.01 _____ Fungi are legumes.

2.02 _____ Water can reach roots by capillary action if the water table is not too deep.

2.03 _____ Carbon dioxide is a waste product of photosynthesis.

2.04 _____ Precipitation is the loss of water by leaves.

2.05 _____ Crop rotation was suggested by George Washington.

2.06 _____ Fungi do not contain chlorophyll.

2.07 _____ The use of hybrid plants can usually increase crop yields.

2.08 _____ Respiration and photosynthesis are basically opposites.

2.09 _____ Aquatic plants do not need sunlight.

2.010 _____ Respiration is the process of utilizing the energy stored in food.

Match these items (each answer, 2 points).

2.011 _____ *Rhizobium*   a. plant breeder

2.012 _____ glucose   b. use of energy in food

2.013 _____ nodule   c. bird waste product

2.014 _____ guard cells   d. crop rotation

2.015 _____ fungi   e. plants without chlorophyll

2.016 _____ Burbank   f. stored carbon

2.017 _____ respiration   g. means *root life*

2.018 _____ guano   h. growth on legume root

2.019 _____ coal   i. green manure

2.020 _____ legume   j. simple sugar

          k. regulate stomata

Write the letter of the correct choice (each answer, 2 points).

2.021 *Rhizobium* bacteria obtain nitrogen from _____ .
   a. proteins   b. nodules   c. legumes   d. soil

2.022 Decay does *not* _____ .
   a. rid the earth of excessive organic matter   b. spoil food
   c. rot wood   d. use chlorophyll

2.023 Thunderstorms provide _____ .
   a. nitrogen compounds   b. carbon dioxide
   c. oxygen   d. urea

2.024 Most of the soil's required nitrogen compounds come from _____ .
   a. *Rhizobium* bacteria   b. compost
   c. manure   d. guano

2.025 The fungi group does *not* include _____ .
   a. yeast   b. molds   c. bacteria   d. mushrooms

2.026 Without decay in the world, plants could grow only as long as _____ .
   a. molds existed   b. guano was formed
   c. proper nutrients were available d. gardeners made compost piles

2.027 The amount of water trapped in polar ice _____ .
   a. changes rapidly   b. is not important
   c. determines the level of the oceans   d. determines the number of polar bears

2.028 The most common compound on earth is _____ .
   a. water   b. oil   c. phosphorus   d. oxygen

2.029 Ground water is _____ .
   a. stored in porous soil and rock   b. part of the nitrogen cycle
   c. unavailable to plants   d. reduced by respiration

2.030 Animals benefit from plants because plants provide _____ .
   a. food and oxygen   b. starch and water
   c. proteins and carbon dioxide   d. nodules and nitrogen

Complete these activities (each answer, 5 points).

2.031 List four legume plants.

a. _____   b. _____

c. _____   d. _____

2.032 Describe the relationship between *Rhizobium* bacteria and legumes.

_____

_____

2.033 Give two reasons that decomposition is so important.

a. _____

b. _____

2.034 List five methods of food preservation and give an example of each.

a. _____   _____

b. _____   _____

c. _____   _____

d. _____   _____

e. _____   _____

56 / 70

SCORE _____   TEACHER _____ _____

initials   date

3. BALANCE AND DISRUPTION

Many recent events have caused a wide public interest in the **environment**. **Ecology** has become a household word and is included in many science courses.

Nature is in balance because of **natural controls** that God established. No one species is present in numbers greater than the environment can handle. This natural balance has been disrupted through population pressures, ignorance, technology. and greed. America has been blessed with an abundance of natural resources such as soil, forests, minerals, fossil fuels, air, water, wildlife, and wilderness. These resources need careful tending if future generations are to have their share of the natural resources of our nation and world. God intends for us to be faithful stewards because "the earth is the LORD's, and the fullness thereof" (Ps. 24:1).

SECTION OBJECTIVES

Review these objectives. When you have completed this section, you should be able to:

11. Define ten ecological terms.
12. Cite four human pressures on the environment and give an example of each.
13. List eight natural resources and give one way of conserving each resource.

VOCABULARY

Study these words to enhance your learning success in this section.

carnivore (kär' nu vôr). An animal that eats only other animals.

community (ku myü' nu tē). A group of animals and plants living in the same area.

ecology (ē kol' u jē). The study of the relationships between organisms and their environment and each other.

environment (en vī' run munt). The surroundings of an organism.

habitat (hab' u tat). The place where an animal or plant naturally lives and grows.

herbivore (hėr' bu vôr). An animal that eats only plants.

natural controls (nach' ur ul kun trōlz'). Conditions that limit the population of an organism.

omnivore (om' nu vôr). An animal that eats both plants and animals.

scavenger (skav' un jur). An animal that eats dead material.

species (spē shēz). A distinct type of animal or plant.

NATURE IN BALANCE

The study of **ecology** has shown the careful balance of nature. Every **community** has all the requirements for existence. Each community also has a series of checks and balances, which insure that no organism will be present in numbers too great for the good of the total **environment**.

Ecology. Ecology is the study of organisms in relationship to their environment. The Greek work *oikos,* meaning *home,* supplied this term to science over 100 years ago. All organisms living in a certain area make up a community. Ecology is usually studied at the community level. A lake, a section of prairie, a seashore, or a forest are examples of communities. A **habitat** is the specific place in the community where an organism lives. If the community is compared to a city, the habitat would be the organism's address. *Community* is a general term, but a *habitat* is specific. A monkey is a member of a jungle community; its habitat is the trees. A gila woodpecker is a common bird of the desert community; its habitat is holes in the saguaro cactus. The habitat of an organism includes the plants, animals, and nonliving things surrounding it. The rainforest habitat of a parrot includes trees, vines, animals, and other birds as well as warm temperatures, heavy rainfall, high humidity, and sunlight. The habitat of a polar bear includes not only fish and seals but also cold temperatures, ice packs, strong winds, and long, dark winters.

Every community must have a source of food that derives its energy from the sun. Plants are called *producers* because they can take energy from the sun and produce food. Grass and other small plants fill this role on the prairie. Algae and aquatic plants provide food in lakes. ponds, and rivers. Trees are a major producer of the jungle: their fruit is a good source for birds and monkeys, and their flowers yield nectar for insects and hummingbirds. Only plants can be producers.

All animals are consumers. Consumers use other organisms as food. If the consumer eats only plants, it is called a **herbivore**. Cattle, mice, deer, and grasshoppers are common land herbivores. Minnows, shrimp, and snails are aquatic herbivores. A **carnivore** is an animal that eats only other animals. Lions, owls, snakes, eagles and alligators are carnivores. A carnivore that eats another carnivore is called a *secondary* carnivore. An animal that is not eaten by any other animal is called the *top* carnivore.

Many animals fall into a group known as **omnivores**. An omnivore eats both plant and animal food. Most humans are omnivores. A strict vegetarian would be classed as a herbivore. Many animals thought to be carnivores have turned out to be omnivores. Wolves and coyotes will eat fruit and berries when supply of mice and rabbits is low.

Decomposers are found throughout the community. Any plant or animal that dies is immediately a food source for the decomposers. The waste materials from all animals is also decomposed by bacteria and fungi into simpler, recyclable units.

Scavengers occupy a special place in the food chain. They feed on dead plants or animals. Vultures, hyenas, and crows are scavengers. They enter the food cycle whenever dead material is available.

In any community the number of plants is far greater than the number of herbivores, and far more herbivores exist than carnivores. This decreasing food availability is called a *food pyramid*. A pyramid results because energy and mass are lost at each level. The pyramid shape results if you count individuals (the *biomass*) at each level, or use the number of calories of energy in each level. Figure 10 is an example of a food pyramid using mass of the organisms at each level. For a human to gain one kilogram, he must consume ten kilograms of fish. One

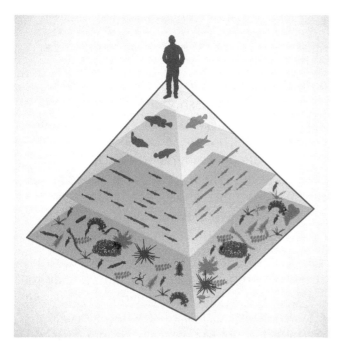

Figure 10 | A Food Pyramid

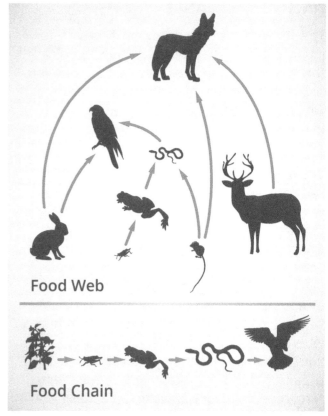

Food Web

Food Chain

Figure 11 | Food Chain and Food Web

hundred kilograms of minnows are required by the fish to increase their mass the required ten kilograms. The minnows would have to consume one thousand kilograms of plants. All this plant material is required to add one kilogram to the mass of a human. A vast amount of plant material must be consumed to support a large animal. The numbers are the same whether the animal eats the plants directly or eats a series of smaller animals that consume the plants. The amount of plants consumed by an animal is easier to calculate if the animal is a herbivore. The elephant is a herbivore and almost destroys the vegetation with its appetite. The American bison herds needed to travel almost constantly in search of fresh pastures because they required so many plants to stay alive.

The list of animals from producer to top carnivore is called a *food chain*. Very few food chains are simple. Usually many animals eat a variety of plants. Herbivores may be food for many different carnivores. A mouse eats the seeds of dozens of plants. The hawk, snake, fox, coyote, cat, owl, and many other carnivores prey on the mouse. Usually the food chain becomes so complicated that it is called a food web.

Natural controls. Even if a community is very complex, no one **species** of plant or animal is allowed to be out of balance. The number of organisms of any type is always within limits that the environment can handle. An area that sustained only a few mice could not be inhabited by a multitude of foxes. In years of good crops, many mice would survive. More young foxes also would survive because of the abundance of mice. The population of mice would be reduced by the extra foxes. After the reduction of the mice, some of the weaker foxes would starve. This system of checks and balances insures that no species is ever in control. No community outside forces are needed to keep the community in balance. **Natural controls** regulate the numbers of each species.

Define these terms.

3.1   producer _____

3.2   consumer _____

3.3   herbivore _____

3.4   carnivore _____

3.5   scavenger _____

3.6   omnivore _____

3.7   natural control _____

3.8   decomposer _____

3.9   top carnivore _____

3.10 habitat _____

3.11 community _____

3.12 ecology _____

The saguaro cactus of the Arizona desert produces millions of seeds in its lifetime. The desert is not covered with these giant cactuses because most of the seeds are eaten by birds and rodents. Those seeds that do sprout are food for herbivores. The prickly pear is another cactus of the desert that does not overrun the environment. A caterpillar feeds on the stems of the prickly pear and keeps the population down. Prickly pears were taken to the deserts of Australia to be used as fences and cattle food. They reproduced rapidly and soon covered 60 million acres. The natural controls had not been studied. Eventually, the caterpillar had to be brought in to control the cactus.

A similar situation occurred in Australia when rabbits were introduced as food and a source of fur. Rabbits are a familiar animal in much of the world but do not occur in excessive numbers. Australia did not have foxes, coyotes, and wolves to serve as natural controls for the rabbits. Soon rabbits were so plentiful they were eating all the vegetation and disrupting the natural controls of the environment. This time a rabbit disease was introduced to stop the population explosion.

A coral reef is one of the most beautiful and colorful places on earth. Many Pacific reefs in the 1960s were disappearing. Scientists studied the reefs and found that starfish were eating the reefs. Starfish are common reef animals and had never been involved in reef destruction before. A close examination of the reef showed that the starfish population was much greater than normal. A beautiful snail was also common in the reef and was collected and sold for its lovely shell. This snail ate starfish eggs as a major part of its diet. The starfish took over the reef when the natural control of the snail was removed. For many years the reef had been in balance with no species in greater numbers than the habitat could support. Ignorance disrupted this balance in a few short years.

One pair of flies could smother the world in three months if all the eggs hatched and lived. A dandelion could carpet the world in one season. If just one bacterium were to reproduce without natural controls, we would drown in bacteria in less than a weekend. Natural controls work to keep all organisms in a healthy balance.

Answer these questions.

3.13   What would happen to the owl population if the number of mice increased?

_____

3.14   What would happen to the mouse population if the number of owls increased?

_____

3.15   What would happen to the mice and the owls if a drought came? _____

_____

3.16   Why does each step of a food pyramid have fewer animals? _____

_____

Complete this activity.

3.17   Put a check in the proper column.

	Producer	Herbivore	Carnivore	Decomposer	Scavenger
a. turkey vulture					
b. algae					
c. cow					
d. mushroom					
e. grasshopper					
f. bacteria					
g. robin					
h. apple tree					
i. hyena					
j. mold					
k. snake					
l. eagle					
m. snail					
n. grass					
o. lion					

3.18   Construct a food pyramid using facts in Figure 10. Use popped popcorn as your units. You will need 1,000 units to represent the plants, 100 for minnows, 10 for the large fish, and 1 for the human being. Plastic bags can be used to contain each step of the pyramid.

TEACHER CHECK _____ _____

initials   date

HUMAN DISRUPTION

Natural controls keep a balance among organisms in a community. Until relatively recently, the human population has been low. Now the world's population is growing, and the environment is being affected more. In many areas the sheer number of humans is causing problems. The technology needed for comfortable living has brought some unpleasant and unexpected results. Human ignorance and greed have brought some unfortunate and unnecessary environmental consequences.

Population. Human population increases are causing changes in the nature of the environment. Ancient people made only a small impact on the land. They gathered food, killed a few small animals, and then frequently moved on. With primitive agriculture and domestic herds, the soil was altered for the first time. Populations were still small; the effects were still minimal. For thousands of years, disease and famine were natural controls on the human population. An increase in population came with the Industrial Revolution and with advances in medicine and agriculture. Human numbers have been increasing ever since.

In 1850 the world population was approximately 1 billion. By 1987 this number had jumped to 5 billion, and by the year 2027 it is expected to double.

The command to have dominion over all the earth, to replenish it, and subdue it was given by God to human beings from the Creation (Gen. 1:26, 28). We alter the environment daily. We have the potential to harm the environment or preserve it.

In 1972 the first United Nations Conference on Human Environment was held in Sweden. This meeting was an indication that world leaders were concerned. Only people have the capacity to alter the environment at will. Only people have minds to develop intelligent approaches to the problem. However, man's basic sin nature is greedy and selfish and will prevent

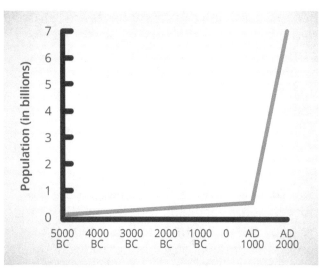

Figure 12 | World Population Growth

a long-term solution. No solution is possible apart from Jesus Christ effecting a change in this basic nature.

Fortunately, disease and famine no longer limit human population growth. The main killers of the past have been conquered by modern medicine. Smallpox, the plague, diphtheria, and scarlet fever no longer take so great a toll. Advances in modern agriculture have increased food supplies. Food can be rushed into areas of potential famine with the aid of rapid transportation. Our recent population growth is as much caused by a decrease in deaths as by an increase in births.

In experimental animal populations, unlimited population growth does not occur. Crowded conditions seem to be mentally unhealthy for the laboratory animals. Mating habits and care of the young are disrupted when the population increases. More young animals die even though food and water are available. When the population drops, normal behavior returns to the animal population.

People in industrialized nations cause a special problem of trash disposal. Ancient people had a few animal bones and inedible fruit parts to discard. That type of garbage readily decomposes, and the components are returned to the soil. Today, the average American discards one ton of trash a year. This garbage is composed mainly of manufactured items that do not readily decompose. Plastic, metal, and paper all create disposal problems. Each person now uses about 225 kilograms of paper each year.

Ignorance. Many ecological disruptions were caused by ignorance. Sometimes people did not foresee what would happen. At other times no one listened to the scientists. Many chose to ignore the findings of scientific studies.

For example, scientists warned that the use of DDT would be very hazardous. DDT killed everything and did not decompose. DDT was sprayed everywhere insects were found because it was such an effective killer. People noticed that fish, birds, and land animals died after an area was sprayed. Bird nests were found empty or with broken eggs. The effect of DDT was not evident for years. Birds ate insects and seeds with DDT spray on them. The DDT did not always kill the adult bird but did disrupt its reproductive cycle. Eggs were not laid or else they had shells so thin that the parent birds broke them in the nest. The bird population fell.

Since DDT does not decompose, it is washed into rivers and streams and carried throughout the world. DDT has been found in penguins of the Antarctic and in milk.

To make matters worse, sometimes the insects returned in even greater numbers. Many insects carried diseases; therefore, world health was in danger when the insect populations increased. Files carry dysentery and eye disease; mosquitoes carry malaria and yellow fever; fleas transmit plague. Resistant strains of insects developed. Each member of an insect population has slightly different characteristics. In any population a few flies, mosquitoes, or fleas were not killed by the DDT. They were less sensitive to the chemical. These members of the insect population were the only ones to survive and reproduce. Their offspring would inherit the parents' resistant traits. When the area was sprayed again, a few of the less sensitive individuals would again survive and reproduce. With time and repeated spraying, all the insects that are sensitive to the DDT would be killed. Only those insects not affected by the DDT would remain. A resistant strain had been developed. This possibility had not been foreseen.

In 1972 almost all uses of DDT were banned by the United Stated government. However, other countries still use DDT so its effects are still being seen in the environment.

Lack of foresight resulted in damage to forests on the north rim of the Grand Canyon. Four thousand mule deer lived there in 1907. The deer were being killed by wolves, coyotes, and mountain lions. The predators were killed so that the deer population could increase. In twenty years the deer population grew close to 100,000 deer. The forest was being destroyed by starving deer. Many deer died. When the natural controls were brought back into the community, the deer population dropped. The forest still shows some damage from this ignorance.

Some hunters make a sport of hunting coyotes in the winter. Coyote tracks are easily seen in the snow, and hunters follow them and shoot the prey. If too many coyotes are killed, rabbits, and mice will eventually multiply in the absence of their natural controls. Human ignorance will have caused another disruption.

Answer these questions.

3.19 What two natural controls have kept human populations low in the past?

a. _____ b. _____

3.20 What three advances have allowed the human population to increase?

a. _____ b. _____ c. _____

3.21 What happens to experimental animals when they become too numerous?

_____

3.22 How does the trash of today differ from that of ancient people?

_____

3.23 What is a *resistant strain*? _____

3.24 What diseases can be carried a. by flies? _____

b. by mosquitoes? _____

c. by fleas? _____

3.25 How does DDT affect bird population? _____

_____

Complete these activities.

3.26 Determine the number of trash containers your family fills up each week. Multiply by 52 to get the figure for one year. Add grass clippings, autumn leaves, and other seasonal trash. Measure your living room. Pretend you had to store all of your trash in the living room for one year. Use mathematics to determine how deep a pile the trash would make.

TEACHER CHECK _____ _____
 initials date

3.27 Use the encyclopedia and write a one-page story on smallpox, diphtheria, scarlet fever, or the plague.

TEACHER CHECK _____ _____
 initials date

Greed. Some stories that relate human disruption of the environment can be traced to greed. For money, sport, or show, people have harmed animal and plant populations. Fur coats made of rare animal skins were highly prized as a sign of wealth. Trophy hunters shot scarce game animals so they could mount animal heads in their homes. Many birds have become endangered because their beautiful feathers were sold. Many nations now forbid the shooting of rare animals, but illegal hunting continues.

The United States and many other nations prohibit the importation of endangered animals and plants, and of any item made from an endangered species. Elephants were hunted for their ivory. The alligator was in danger of extinction in the United States because its hide made excellent shoes and purses. Alligator products were taken off the market, and now the population of alligators has increased.

The desert has been damaged by persons who dig cactuses, pot them, and sell them. Cactuses grow so slowly that a large plant is expensive. State laws now forbid removal of cactuses.

The government had long rewarded farmers for planting rows of trees or shelter belts to stop the wind and prevent erosion. When grain prices were high, some farmers removed the trees that the government had paid them to plant. Removing the trees gave the farmer a few more acres of grain, which would give them a few more dollars.

Some people want to buy rare, imported birds and animals for pets. United States customs officials discover smugglers bringing in these birds and animals for the pet market. Many of the animals die for each one that arrives in the United States alive. The smuggler makes a good profit on the pets because the animals are purchased cheaply in the jungle. Greed made the smuggler bring in the animals. Greed makes the buyer want a rare creature that very few other people have.

Newspapers often have accounts of huge tracts of land sold for homesites. The land is landscaped, and much of the vegetation is removed. The developer clears the land and divides it into small plots. Little time is taken to preserve the trees and plants when roads are constructed. The practice gives far more profit to the developers.

Technology. Technology has made life easier for everyone. Technology has brought more nutritious food, better clothing, faster transportation, comfortable homes, and hundreds of other advances that make our life easier, longer, happier, and healthier. Technology has also brought some unexpected consequences. Each advance must be studied to make certain that the bad does not outweigh the good.

Agricultural chemicals have increased food production manyfold. Unfortunately, some human deaths have been caused by exposure to these chemicals. At times, chemicals have been made that are dangerous to store and are difficult to destroy. Dangerous chemicals have been buried in holes drilled in Colorado and Alaska. Earthquakes hit those areas in abnormal numbers after the chemicals were placed in the ground. The liquids may have expanded the rocks and released an earthquake. In other areas the buried chemicals have leaked out of the ground.

Mercury compounds were used extensively until mercury was found in tuna fish far from the source of the mercury. Mercury causes illness, paralysis, and mental deterioration in humans. Long ago, mercury was used to manufacture felt for men's hats. Those who made hats usually suffered. The effects of mercury poisoning on people who made hats were the origin of the phrase "mad as a hatter."

At times, chemicals not only harm the environment but also do not do the intended job. The development of DDT-resistant insects is one example. At other times, one insect may be destroyed by a spray, but a far more injurious insect will take its place. The Japanese beetle was causing damage to corn crops in Illinois. The fields were sprayed, and the beetle disappeared. Unfortunately, the far more damaging corn borer was food for the Japanese beetle. With the beetle gone, the corn-borer population increased and did far more damage than the Japanese beetle would have caused.

 Complete this activity.

3.28 Look up "Environmental Pollution" in an encyclopedia and read about how technology affects the environment. Read about water and soil pollution. Watch for articles in magazines or newspapers about the problems of pollution. What effects does pollution have? Write a one-page summary of your reading.

TEACHER CHECK _____ _____
                                              initials   date

Answer these questions.

3.29 How has each of these organisms been used for profit?

a. elephant _____

b. alligator _____

c. leopard _____

d. cactuses _____

e. lion _____

f. beautiful birds _____

3.30 Why did corn borers increase after a field was sprayed for Japanese beetles?

_____

3.31 What are three advantages of technology? a. _____

b. _____ , c. _____

Complete these activities.

3.32 State three problems of technology.

a. _____

b. _____

c. _____

3.33 List the four types of human disruptions covered in the LIFEPAC and write an example of each.

a. _____

b. _____

c. _____

d. _____

RESOURCES

Our nation has been blessed with an abundance of natural resources. Most resources have been affected by the population pressures and technological advances of our country. Minerals, fossil fuels, air, water, soil, forests, wildlife, and wilderness areas all need to be studied and conserved so that we are good stewards of these natural resources.

Soil and forests. The basis of any community is its soil and plants. Plants could not survive without soil and the nutrients it contains. Animals could not exist without plants as the producers of food.

Many years are required to make one centimeter of good topsoil. When the United States was settled, topsoil thickness averaged 22 centimeters. Today, 15 centimeters remain.

When plants are removed from the soil, the eroding forces of wind and rain take their toll. Some erosion always occurs. Farming and the clearing of forests accelerates the process. Land that has been cleared for farming lies unprotected from harvest until planting. Shelter belts of trees help stop the wind and hold moisture. Plowing along the natural contours of hills slows the rainfall that would wash the soil away. Ancient people often built terraces on hillsides to protect the soil from erosion and provide additional growing space. The rice terraces of the Philippines are ancient but are still usable because of good care. The Incas of South America increased crop areas and prevented erosion by constructing elaborate terraces.

Sprays used to kill insects and weeds affect bacteria of the soil. Since *Rhizobium* bacteria are responsible for soil fertility, we must use caution. The land could be harmed by a chemical that was meant to destroy only an insect or weed.

When the United States was settled, over one-third of the land was covered with forests. Forests are a renewable resource. Lumber and paper companies are active in planting forests for future use. These forests will provide lumber and paper pulp but are usually not as varied as the original forests. The wide variety of trees and plants in virgin forests provides a number of different habitats for wildlife that are missing from the replanted forests. Forest areas provide hiking, camping, hunting, and nature study for millions of people.

Forest fires have always been caused by lightning, but now humans are the major cause of forest fires. A study showed that arson accounted for 24 percent of the forest fires, trash burning out of control was responsible for 23 percent of the fires, and careless smokers ignited 18 percent of the blazes.

Forests are important in communications. Paper is made from wood pulp and used for books, magazines, and newspapers. Newspapers are heavy users of the forest. Just one daily edition of a New York newspaper takes 44 acres of trees. Lumber companies efficiently cut large trees for lumber and use the branches and waste sections for paper pulp.

Conserving the soil and forests is an important project. Paper can be recycled for home insulation or for new paper products. Since most forest fires have human origins, caution must be used when in or near forested areas. One second of carelessness can wipe out the growth of many years. Proper agricultural and forestry practices are vital to the future of soil and forests.

Minerals and fossil fuels. No way is presently known to renew minerals and fossil fuels once the present supply is gone. Plastics have taken the place of some metal products; but plastics are produced from fossil fuels, which also are diminishing.

Industry has long realized that the supply of minerals is decreasing. Already ores are used that were once overlooked because of their low yield. *Recycling* is the reuse of old materials in the process of making products. Recycling is expensive but does conserve resources. About 60 percent of each year's copper production is from recycled copper. Fifty percent of aluminum is recycled. Approximately 25 percent of the steel manufactured is recycled from scrap iron. Glass is also recycled but presents a special problem. Each color and type of glass needs to be sorted and separated. Improved technology is needed to speed up this process to make glass recycling more economical.

Fossil fuels, the remains of ancient plants and animals, include gas, oil, and coal. These fuels are the energy source for automobiles, factories, and electrical generating plants. Since the sun is the only renewable energy source, the rate of depletion of fossil fuels must be watched closely. The United States is a heavy user of energy. The United States of America makes up only 6 percent of the world population but uses 26 percent of the energy.

Fossil fuel molecules are also the basis of the plastic industry. Other forms of energy are being sought so fossil fuel supplies can be reserved for plastic manufacturing. The sun, wind, and atomic energy are all being investigated as possible energy substitutes. Atomic energy has some health, safety, and environmental problems that need to be considered before it can become a major energy source. The possibility of nuclear accidents and radiation damage must be reduced to protect people and the environment.

Nuclear reactors use large amounts of water for cooling. Some of this water is returned to the environment after it is used. Warm water will not absorb as much oxygen as normally cool water, so fish and other aquatic organisms are affected. The warm water also acts as a barrier to fish such as the salmon when they migrate upstream to their spawning grounds.

Windmills require a lot of steel to build them and it can take some time to recover the manufacturing cost with the energy produced if they are not placed in a good location. Constant strong winds are rare even in areas that seem especially windy. Solar energy has potential for home use and is receiving much governmental support. Although the sun has plentiful energy even in winter, the needs for heat are greatest in the north where winter days are short. Current solar energy equipment is expensive. Improved technology and mass production normally lower prices.

New energy sources must be perfected so that fossil fuels can be conserved. Inexpensive and readily available energy has been a major reason why our globe can support so many people. Problems will arise as energy becomes less available and as underdeveloped nations require more.

Conservation of minerals and fossil fuels seems easy until translated into personal concerns. People might consider walking to save fuel. Small cars or public transportation can be used when distances are vast. Driving older cars and bicycles will save the energy needed to recycle the metal for parts. Machines and tools could be repaired instead of discarding and replacing them. Much fossil fuel is used for disposable plastic bags and bottles. New methods of recycling are being developed to make new products out of many items that are commonly discarded. God has given human beings wonderful abilities to use the resources provided by the earth.

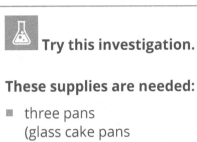 **Try this investigation.**

These supplies are needed:

- three pans (glass cake pans work fine)
- sprinkling can
- soil
- ruler
- grass seed
- water

Follow these directions and complete the activity. Put a check in the box when each step is completed.

☐ 1. Fill the three pans with soil.

☐ 2. Plant each pan with the rows 2 centimeters apart.
Pan 1. Plant grass in rows across the width of the pan.
Pan 2. Plant grass in rows that go the length of the pan.
Pan 3. Plant no grass.

☐ 3. Water the pans and place them in bright light. Care for them until the grass is 3 centimeters tall.

☐ 4. Take the pans outside and prop them up so one end is 10 centimeters off the ground. Use the sprinkling can and give each pan an equally heavy watering. Observe the amount of soil erosion in each pan.

3.34 Write a paragraph telling how your experiment would be valuable information for a farmer who owned hilly land.

TEACHER CHECK _____ _____
initials   date

Soil Erosion Experiment

Answer these questions.

3.35 What two unfortunate things are happening to our soil?

a. _____

b. _____

3.36 How does farming expose soil to erosion? _____

_____

3.37 What five things do forests provide?

a. _____   b. _____

c. _____   d. _____

e. _____

3.38 What three metals are commonly recycled?

a. _____   b. _____   c. _____

3.39 What are three common fossil fuels?

a. _____   b. _____   c. _____

3.40 What is the origin of fossil fuels? _____

3.41 What two industries are the main users of fossil fuels?

a. _____   b. _____

Complete this activity.

3.42 List three alternate energy sources and one problem of each.

a. _____

b. _____

c. _____

_____

Air and water. When settlers first came to the United States, the air was clean. Drinking water could be dipped from any lake or stream. Now supplies of pure air and water are in danger. Only one percent of the water of the world is in a salt-free form that plants and animals can use. Any pollution of this one percent may affect the quality of life.

Rising water vapor condenses on any available nuclei at cooler temperatures in the upper atmosphere. These nuclei can be auto exhaust, poisonous molecules, or smoke.

When precipitation falls, these pollutants are brought down into the water supply. Some industrial areas of the world have experienced black snow. Samples of fresh snow taken from remote regions of North America contain lead from auto exhaust.

The oceans have been used for garbage disposal. Some coastal cities dump sewage into the ocean. Sailors report that floating trash occurs frequently in the ocean. Clumps of oil residues are found in all global waters. The number of fish species is dropping.

Supertankers have brought new problems to the ocean. Millions of gallons of oil are spilled in every disaster. The spill is carried by ocean currents to areas far away. Fish, birds, and microscopic organisms in the vicinity of the spill are harmed by the oil.

Modern living uses a large quantity of water. An average bath takes 120 liters, and to flush a toilet 24 liters. The water used by industry is used because the consumer demands the product. A new bicycle takes 2,600 liters of water in the various manufacturing processes.

Some pure water is wasted each year. In the 1950 water shortage in New York, engineers estimated that 200 million gallons of water were lost just through leaky faucets. Taking a pitcher of cold water from the refrigerator is more efficient than letting the tap run each time a drink is needed. Showers could be shorter without sacrificing cleanliness. Sailors learn to shower with just a few liters of water.

Ground water is being polluted in some areas. Chemical fertilizers and wastes from livestock pens have washed into some water systems and caused illness. In cold climates where salt is used on icy roads, the salt might seep into the ground water. Persons with heart problems must buy special drinking water. We are pumping water out of the ground 140 times faster than precipitation is flowing back into the system. Along coastal areas, salty seawater is being drawn into water supplies. The ground water is becoming too salty for irrigation.

The air is being polluted. The private auto causes 60 percent of the pollution in the air. The remainder is caused by factories and electrical generating plants.

Our atmosphere is in danger also because we are polluting the ocean. Chemical pollution is affecting the small microscopic plants of the ocean. These tiny producers are the basis for all life of the ocean. Ocean plants also give off about 50 percent of the oxygen released by photosynthesis. This oxygen is an important part of our atmosphere. A 17-by-17-meter plot of grass is needed to provide the oxygen for a family of four. This same amount of oxygen is quickly used by driving a car just a few blocks. Walking, biking, and mass transit consume less oxygen and yield fewer pollutants.

Wildlife and wilderness. The impact upon the wildlife was one of the first events that focused attention on the problems of pollution. People would report dead birds, fish, and small animals just hours after an area had been sprayed for insects or weeds. Even though few people rely on hunting for food, animals and birds are important. Bird watching is a fast-growing hobby. More fishing licenses are sold each year. Nature study has become a favorite recreation.

Sometimes animals provide more than just enjoyment. The hippopotamus population in Africa was purposely reduced. Shortly afterwards, an increase was noted in a disease spread by a snail. The hippo had kept down this disease by its habit of walking through the streams. The large bodies of the hippo created open passages for the water to quickly flow downstream. When the hippos were killed, the streams filled in, and the water overflowed. The disease-bearing snails thrived in this still water. The ecology of any habitat is very complex, and the disruption of any one species could have unexpected consequences.

Approximately 1,200 species are now on the endangered list. An organism is considered endangered when its numbers fall so low that it is in danger of becoming extinct. In the past 400 years about 225 species are known to have become extinct. Human pressure on the environment played a major role in at least three-fourths of the cases. Many plants have disappeared in the same amount of time. Countless orchid species become extinct in the jungles of Central America each year as the jungle is cleared for farm land. Some plants become extinct even before they can be discovered and named.

Each year millions of visitors visit national parks and other wilderness areas. Such scenic areas repay citizens many times over with their beauty. More money is needed for recreational areas.

Some people suggest a policy similar to the Pittman-Robertson Act of 1937. Two congressmen organized a bill that allowed an 11 percent tax on guns and ammunition. These funds were used to purchase hunting grounds and conduct research on game management. A similar tax has been suggested for boats, hiking boots, tents, and other outdoor gear to finance wilderness and wildlife projects.

 Answer these questions.

3.43 What two things are happening to the ground water?

a. _____

b. _____

3.44 What percentage of air pollution is caused by the automobile?

_____

3.45 What are two important reasons for protecting microscopic ocean plants?

a. _____

b. _____

3.46 In what way does the automobile alter the atmosphere?

a. _____   b. _____

3.47 Why are wild birds and animals important to many people? _____

_____

Complete these activities.

3.48 Consult five of your classmates and make a list of any hobbies they have that make use of wildlife or the wilderness. You will probably find bird watching, fishing, hunting, hiking, camping, photography, canoeing, and many other hobbies on your list.

Share the list with your teacher.

TEACHER CHECK _____ _____
                                            initials   date

3.49 Find out the name of an endangered species that lives in your area of the country. The Department of Game and Fish or the local chapter of the Audubon Society will be able to help you. Write a page about the animal or plant. Include the reason for the decline of the population.

3.50 List the eight major natural resources and one way we can conserve each of them.

a. _____   _____

b. _____   _____

c. _____   _____

d. _____   _____

e. _____   _____

f. _____   _____

g. _____   _____

h. _____   _____

TEACHER CHECK _____ _____
                                            initials   date

Before you take this last Self Test, you may want to do one or more of these self checks.

1. _____ Read the objectives. See if you can do them.
2. _____ Restudy the material related to any objectives that you cannot do.
3. _____ Use the **SQ3R** study procedure to review the material:
   a. **S**can the sections.
   b. **Q**uestion yourself.
   c. **R**ead to answer your questions.
   d. **R**ecite the answers to yourself.
   e. **R**eview areas you did not understand.
4. _____ Review all vocabulary, activities, and Self Tests, writing a correct answer for every wrong answer.

SELF TEST 3

Write true or false (each answer, 1 point).

3.01 _____ Plants may become extinct even before they are discovered or named.

3.02 _____ Trace elements are required for plant growth.

3.03 _____ Starch is usually missing from the diet of underdeveloped nations.

3.04 _____ Only humans have the capacity to alter the environment at will.

3.05 _____ Fungi are a class of legumes.

3.06 _____ A cow is a producer.

3.07 _____ Chloroplasts are found in leaf epidermal cells only.

3.08 _____ Glucose is a simple sugar.

3.09 _____ Deer are natural controls for wolves and coyotes.

3.010 _____ Some strains of insects have become resistant to DDT.

Complete these sentences (each answer, 3 points).

3.011 The study of organisms in relation to their environment is called _____ .

3.012 Fresh water available for plants and animals to use is only _____ percent of the total water on earth.

3.013 A cross between two unlike varieties of plants or animal is called a _____ .

3.014 A food pyramid has fewer animals at each level because of the loss of _____ .

3.015 If you want to find a root nodule, you would have to look for a plant that was a

_____ .

3.016 Alternating crops on different fields is called _____ .

3.017 The private auto accounts for _____ percent of the pollution in the air.

3.018 The three elements commonly found in bags of fertilizer are phosphorous, potassium, and

_____ .

3.019 In the food web, a turkey vulture is an example of a _____ .

3.020 Animal respiration provides plants with _____ .

Match these items (each answer, 2 points).

3.021	_____ fossil fuel	a.	producer
3.022	_____ animal	b.	where an organism lives
3.023	_____ transpiration	c.	nitrogen-fixing
3.024	_____ ecology	d.	green pigment
3.025	_____ *Rhizobium*	e.	ancient plants and animals
3.026	_____ chlorophyll	f.	stored in porous rock
3.027	_____ plant	g.	water loss
3.028	_____ respiration	h.	consumer
3.029	_____ habitat	i.	polar ice
3.030	_____ ground water	j.	use of energy in food
		k.	relationship of organisms to their environment

Write the letter of the correct answer on each line (each answer, 2 points).

3.031 Ground water is becoming _____ .
   a. depleted and warmer
   b. polluted and radioactive
   c. polluted and depleted
   d. increased and salty

3.032 Humans have been responsible for what percent of the extinct species? _____ .
   a. 25%   b. 95%   c. 75%   d. 50%

3.033 Three alternate energy sources are _____ .
   a. sun, wind, rain
   b. atomic energy, coal, wind
   c. coal, oil, gas
   d. sun, wind, atomic energy

3.034 Human disruption of the environment is *not* caused by _____ .
   a. greed
   b. natural controls
   c. population
   d. technology and ignorance

3.035 In the past, human populations were controlled by _____ .
   a. wolves and coyotes
   b. disease and famine
   c. disease and pollution
   d. greed and ignorance

3.036 The special cells that regulate the openings of stomata are called _____ .
   a. epidermal cells
   b. stoma
   c. guard cells
   d. inner cells

3.037 The major groups of decomposers are _____ .
   a. algae and bacteria
   b. scavengers and predators
   c. bacteria and fungi
   d. carbon and oxygen

3.038 In photosynthesis the carbon dioxide comes from _____ .
- a. animal respiration
- b. the light phase
- c. the dark phase
- d. legume root nodules

3.039 The oxygen formed during photosynthesis is considered a _____ .
- a. waste product
- b. trace mineral
- c. fertilizer
- d. nutrient

3.040 Modern agriculture was made possible by machines, farm chemicals, and _____ .
- a. increased yields
- b. disease resistance
- c. hybrid plants
- d. special characteristics

Define these terms (each answer, 3 points).

3.041 ecology _____

3.042 habitat _____

3.043 producer _____

3.044 consumer _____

3.045 community _____

3.046 carnivore _____

3.047 herbivore _____

3.048 natural control _____

3.049 omnivore _____

3.050 scavenger _____

Complete these lists (each lettered item, 3 points).

3.051 List eight natural resources and one way of conserving each.

a. _____   _____

b. _____   _____

c. _____   _____

d. _____   _____

e. _____   _____

f. _____   _____

g. _____   _____

h. _____   _____

3.052 List four human disruptions of the environment. Give an example of each one.

a. _____   _____

b. _____   _____

c. _____   _____

d. _____   _____

Before taking the LIFEPAC Test, you may want to do one or more of these self checks.

1. _____ Read the objectives. See if you can do them.
2. _____ Restudy the material related to any objectives that you cannot do.
3. _____ Use the **SQ3R** study procedure to review the material.
4. _____ Review activities, Self Tests, and LIFEPAC vocabulary words.
5. _____ Restudy areas of weakness indicated by the last Self Test.